the Children's
food & drink party book

R&R PUBLICATIONS MARKETING PTY LTD

R&R Publications Marketing Pty Ltd
12 Edward Street, Brunswick
Victoria 3056, Australia
Phone (61 3) 9381 2199 Fax (61 3) 9381 2689
Australia-wide toll free 1800 063 296
E-mail: info@randrpublications.com.au
Web: www.randrpublications.com.au

Publisher: Richard Carroll
Designer: Aisling Gallagher
Food Editor: Neil Hargreaves
Photographer: Brent Parker Jones
Food Stylist: Neil Hargreaves
Presentation: R&R PhotoStudio
Proofreader: Sandra Goldbloom Zurbo

ISBN: 1 74022 597 X
EAN: 9 781740 225977

Published: October 2006
Printed in China by
Max Production Printing Ltd

Cover image: Strawberry Swirl, page 81

Contents

Introduction 5

Fruit Combos 13

Novelty Drinks 45

For the Curious 83

Party Snacks 95

Index 128

Smoothie Origins

Many of the drinks in *The Children's food and party book* are smoothie-style drinks. Smoothies deserve a quick introduction.

Smoothies, a drink made of fruit and, often, yogurt and honey are reminiscent of traditional old-world drinks of India and the Middle East. Many early Hindu offerings in drink form contain honey and yogurt. So, the smoothie has been around in different forms for a long time.

Earliest known smoothie recipes in the West date back to Los Angeles in the 1920s, but it wasn't until the 1970s that smoothies began to be seen as a healthy alternative to milkshakes – being primarily fresh fruit based, and sometimes containing a little milk and yogurt, not all dairy, including ice cream, and flavored syrups. By the 1990s, smoothie bars could be found everywhere.

In *The Children's food and party book*, we have started with a few simple classics to get you rolling, fruit combinations that are very popular at smoothie bars and juice bars. These are followed by more novel and festive recipes that are fun and playful combinations for the day of the party.

The Children's food and party book finishes up with more complicated combinations, recipes for the older and more adventurous children and the young at heart. After all, why should the kids have all the fun!

Getting Organized

Take the time to taste your first drink, particularly if you are making a few batches for a party of children, and remember to adjust the amount of sweeteners you are using. This will depend upon the season. Most fruits are sweeter at different times of the year; they are more luscious and hold more moisture when they are in season. It is worth having a look at the markets to see what is on offer and be guided by what is abundant at the time. Not only will your fruit be sweeter but it will taste better and be cheaper when it is in season.

In most of these recipes you can easily add more ice to mellow out the flavors and make your drinks go further or, for a stronger flavored slushie-style of drink, you can deseed and peel your fruits, then cut them into ice-sized cubes. Do this ahead of time. Lay them out in the freezer (on trays or in ice trays rather than bowls so they do not end up as one large block when frozen). This bit of extra planning keeps you more organized and cleaner. You can freeze your fruits a long way ahead of time and even prepare and freeze fruit that will be out of season on the day of the party.

Some Basic Tips

Limit the sticky stuff such as ice cream and lollies, for later so things don't get too messy too early. Some people like the lollie bag-on-exit policy so the children are not running around, en masse, in a sugar frenzy.

It is also a good thing to politely reinforce manners while you have a group of little ones on hand. Good manners can make for a little more control and the day less likely to see bouts of tears if there is a degree of restraint and an expectation that everybody is to be considerate.

Involve your children in a little of the planning and see which activities inspire them and which they seem less interested in and plan accordingly.

Consider your numbers. A party for the entire grade at school can easily become a semi-professional event to manage on the day. Consider the time span of your party and adjust according to the age of the children. A party can be as exhausting as it is exciting for the little ones, so keep yourself to schedule and finish up your party with some slightly lower impact games and experiences.

Keep Them Busy

Keep the list of games to a maximum so if something does not work out you can quickly swing into the next activity. Here is a quick checklist of games to get you thinking about which activities you think the children will enjoy.

Charades	**Ring-a-ring of Roses**
Chinese Whispers	**Round the Mulberry Bush**
Freeze	**Simon Says**
Hide and Seek	**Egg and Spoon Race**
Musical Chairs	**Treasure Hunt**
Pass the Parcel	**Tug of War**
Pin the Tail on the Donkey	**What's the Time, Mr Wolf?**

Ok. Drinks, games, lollie policy. All that's left to remind you about is to always have a party buddy. This is not the day to be the solo operator of cakes, candles, presents, tears, band-aids and hugs. You are going to need some help. Oh, and remember to enjoy the day yourself and to take plenty of happy snap photographs.

Raspberry Orange Delight (page 78)

Fruit Combo's

Banana Smoothie 14

Banapple Smoothie 14

Banberry Smoothie 14

Berry Banana Smoothie 19

Banana Zing Smoothie 19

Calypso Smoothie 19

Custard Apple Smoothie 22

Fruit Salad Smoothie 22

Grape Slushie Swirl 22

Hawaiian Delight Smoothie 27

Kiwi Frootz Smoothie 27

Mango and Orange Smoothie 27

Mango Morning Smoothie 30

Melon Mix Smoothie 30

Passion Frootz 30

Strawberry Orange Banana Smoothie 35

Strawberry Smoothie 35

Sunrise Surprise Smoothie 35

Tropical Burst Smoothie 38

Tropical Frootz Smoothie 38

Tropical Zing Smoothie 38

Tropicana Smoothie 43

Tropico Blitz 43

Banana Smoothie

½ cup milk
1½ bananas
½ cup plain yogurt
1 tsp honey

2–3 drops vanilla extract
sprinkle of nutmeg (optional)
4 ice cubes

Place all ingredients except nutmeg in blender; blend until smooth.
Pour into chilled glasses and serve topped with a sprinkle of nutmeg.
Serves 2.

Banapple Smoothie

½ cup milk
½ banana
½ apple, peeled
½ cup plain yogurt

1 tsp honey
2–3 drops vanilla extract
3 ice cubes
purple sprinkles to garnish

Place all ingredients except sprinkles in blender; blend until smooth.
Pour into chilled glasses and serve. Serves 2.

Banberry Smoothie

½ cup milk
½ banana
2 strawberries
½ apple, peeled

5–6 blueberries
½ cup plain yogurt
1 tsp honey
3 ice cubes

Place all ingredients in blender; blend until smooth, Pour into chilled
glasses and serve topped with coloured sprinkles. Serves 2.

Banana Smoothie

Banapple Smoothie

Banberry Smoothie

Berry Banana Smoothie

Berry Banana Smoothie

½ cup milk
1 banana
6 frozen strawberries
10–12 blueberries

1 tsp honey
2 drops of vanilla extract
vanilla sugar
4 ice cubes

Place all ingredients except sugar in blender; blend until smooth. Pour into chilled glasses and serve topped with a fresh strawberry, a few blueberries and a sprinkle of vanilla sugar. Serves 2.

Banana Zing Smoothie

½ cup milk
½ banana
juice of 1 orange
3–4 drops lemon juice

½ cup plain yogurt
2 tsps apple juice concentrate
2 slices of orange
4 ice cubes

Place all ingredients except orange slices in blender; blend until smooth. Pour into chilled glasses and serve topped with a slice of orange. Serves 2.

Calypso Smoothie

½ cup milk
⅓ cup pineapple
pulp of 2 passionfruit
½ banana

½ cup plain yogurt
1 tsp honey
extra passionfruit pulp to garnish
4 ice cubes

Place all ingredients, except garnish in blender; blend until smooth. Pour into chilled glasses and serve with a swirl of passionfruit to garnish. Serves 2.

Banana Zing Smoothie

Calypso Smoothie

Custard Apple Smoothie

½ cup milk
½ cup custard apple, deseeded
½ banana
½ cup plain yogurt

1 tsp honey
2 drops vanilla extract
nutmeg
4 ice cubes

Place all ingredients, except nutmeg in blender; blend until smooth. Pour into chilled glasses and serve topped with a sprinkle of nutmeg. Serves 2.

Fruit Salad Smoothie

½ cup milk
⅓ cup of pineapple
2 strawberries
⅓ banana

⅓ apple, peeled
½ cup plain yogurt
1 tsp honey
4 ice cubes

Place all ingredients in blender; blend until smooth. Pour into chilled glasses and serve. Serves 2.

Grape Slushie Swirl

1 cup seedless red grapes, frozen
1 cup seedless green grapes, frozen
¼ tsp fresh ginger pulp

2 tbsps fig jelly
1 tsp white sugar
2 ice blocks

Blend 1 ice block, green grapes, ginger pulp and sugar in blender until slushy and all combined. Spoon out into a chilled bowl and place in freezer. Blend the other ice block, red grapes and fig jelly until slushy and all combined. Spoon out into a chilled bowl. Collect green grape slushie and spoon each coloured mixture into serving glasses, a few scoops of each colour at a time until glasses are full. Serves 2.

Custard Apple Smoothie

Fruit Salad Smoothie

Grape Slushie Swirl

Hawaiian Delight Smoothie

Hawaiian Delight Smoothie

½ cup milk
6 cherries
½ cup pineapple
½ mandarin
½ cup plain yogurt

1 tsp honey
2–3 drops vanilla extract
pink sprinkles
2 ice cubes

Place all ingredients except sprinkles in blender; blend until smooth.
Pour into chilled glasses and serve topped with coloured sprinkles.
Serves 2.

Kiwi Frootz Smoothie

½ cup milk
½ banana
2 frozen strawberries
1½ peeled kiwifruit
½ cup plain yogurt

2 tsps honey
4 ice cubes
extra kiwifruit and banana to garnish
½ tsp vanilla sugar

Place all ingredients except garnish in blender; blend until smooth.
Pour into chilled glasses and serve topped with a slice of fresh
kiwifruit and banana. Serves 2.

Mango and Orange Smoothie

½ cup milk
pulp of 1 mango
juice of 1 orange
½ cup plain yogurt

1 tsp honey
pinch of cinnamon
2 ice cubes

Place all ingredients except cinnamon in blender; blend until
smooth. Pour into chilled glasses and serve topped with a sprinkle of
cinnamon. Serves 2.

Kiwi Frootz Smoothie

Mango and Orange Smoothie

Mango Morning Smoothie

½ cup milk
½ mango
¼ banana
½ cup plain yogurt

2 tsps toasted muesli
1 tbsp date paste
3 ice cubes

Place all ingredients in blender; blend until smooth. Pour into chilled glasses and serve topped with a sprinkle of muesli. Serves 2.

Melon Mix Smoothie

¼ cup milk
⅓ banana
½ cup watermelon, deseeded
½ cup cantaloupe

½ cup plain yogurt
1 tsp honey
2–3 drops vanilla extract
3 ice cubes

Freeze melon. Place all other ingredients in blender; blend until smooth. Pour into chilled glasses and serve topped with chunks of frozen melon. Serves 2.

Passion Frootz

½ cup milk
½ apple
½ banana
juice of 1 orange

pulp of 1 passionfruit
½ cup plain yogurt
extra passionfruit pulp to garnish
1 tsp honey

Place all ingredients except garnish in blender; blend until smooth. Pour into chilled glasses and serve topped with a swirl of passionfruit pulp. Serves 2.

Mango Morning Smoothie

Melon Mix Smoothie

Passion Frootz

Strawberry Orange Banana Smoothie

Strawberry Orange Banana Smoothie

½ cup milk
1 orange, peeled and deseeded
½ banana
2 strawberries

½ cup plain yogurt
1 tsp honey
2–3 drops vanilla extract
2 ice cubes

Place all ingredients in blender; blend until smooth. Pour into chilled glasses and serve. Serves 2.

Strawberry Smoothie

½ cup milk
6 frozen strawberries
½ cup plain yogurt
1 tsp honey

2–3 drops vanilla extract
pinch of nutmeg (optional)
extra strawberry to garnish
4 blocks of ice

Place all ingredients except garnish in blender; blend until smooth. Pour into chilled glasses and serve topped with half a fresh strawberry. Serves 2.

Sunrise Surprise Smoothie

1 blood orange, peeled and deseeded
pulp of ½ mango
pulp of 2 passionfruit
½ cup plain yogurt
1 tsp honey
2–3 drops vanilla extract
extra yogurt and passionfruit to garnish
4 ice cubes

Place all ingredients except garnishes in blender; blend until smooth. Pour into chilled glasses and serve topped with an extra dollop of yogurt and some passionfruit pulp. Serves 2.

Strawberry Smoothie

Sunrise Surprise Smoothie

Tropical Burst Smoothie

¼ cup milk
1 kiwifruit, peeled and quartered
3 strawberries
½ cup of watermelon, deseeded
½ cup plain yogurt
1 tsp honey
2 ice cubes

Place all ingredients in blender; blend until smooth. Pour into chilled glasses and serve. Serves 2.

Tropical Frootz Smoothie

½ cup milk
½ banana
2 strawberries
½ cup pineapple
½ cup plain yogurt

1 tsp honey
½ cup coconut milk
extra strawberries to garnish
2 ice cubes

Place all ingredients except garnish in blender; blend until smooth. Pour in ½ cup of coconut milk and stir. Pour into chilled glasses and serve topped with strawberries. Serves 2.

Tropical Zing Smoothie

⅓ cup milk
½ orange
¼ mango
pulp of 2 passionfruit

½ cup pineapple
½ cup plain yogurt
1 tsp honey
2 ice cubes

Reserve some passionfruit. Place all other ingredients in blender; blend until smooth. Pour into chilled glasses and serve topped with passionfruit. Serves 2.

Tropical Burst Smoothie

Tropical Frootz Smoothie

Tropical Zing Smoothie

Tropicana Smoothie

Tropicana Smoothie

½ cup milk
½ mango
½ banana
½ apple
2 strawberries
extra strawberry to garnish
¼ cup plain yogurt
1 tsp honey
3 ice cubes

Place all ingredients except garnish in blender; blend until smooth.
Pour into chilled glasses and serve topped with a fanned strawberry.
Serves 2.

Tropico Blitz

1 small ripe banana, sliced
1 cup frozen peach slices
½ cup orange juice
2 tbsps fresh lime juice
2 tbsps honey
4 drops vanilla extract
¼ tsp ground cinnamon
2 ice blocks

Place all ingredients except cinnamon in blender; blend until
smooth. Pour into chilled glasses and serve topped with a sprinkle of
cinnamon. Serves 2.

Tropico Blitz

Novelty Drinks

Anzac Cookie Smoothie **46**

Apple Cherry Pie Smoothie **46**

Apple Crumble Smoothie **46**

Apricot Danish Smoothie **51**

Banana Berry Muffin Smoothie **51**

Banana Cherry Split Smoothie **51**

Banana Choc Nut Smoothie **54**

Banana Pudding Smoothie **54**

Banario Smoothie **54**

Cheesecake Smoothie **59**

Cherry Ripe Smoothie **59**

Choc Berry Smoothie **59**

Choc Mint Berry Smoothie **62**

Honey Smack Smoothie **62**

Honeydew Heaven **62**

Iced Vovo Smoothie **67**

Jaffa Smoothie **67**

Lemon Meringue Smoothie **67**

Lucious Lime Pie Smoothie **70**

Monte Carlo Smoothie **70**

Muesli (Granola) Bar Smoothie **70**

Peanut Butter and Jelly Smoothie **75**

Pear and Coconut Delight Smoothie **75**

Pear Danish Smoothie **75**

Raspberry Orange Delight **78**

Strawberry Shortcake Smoothie **78**

Strawberry Swirl **81**

Toffee Apple Smoothie **81**

Anzac Cookie Smoothie

½ cup milk
½ cup plain yogurt
½ cup stewed or roasted pear, chilled
½ cup toasted granola

extra toasted granola to garnish
2 tsps corn syrup
3 drops of vanilla extract
3 ice cubes

Place all ingredients except garnish in blender; blend until smooth. Pour into chilled glasses and serve topped with extra granola. Serves 2.

Apple Cherry Pie Smoothie

½ cup milk
2 strawberries
3 cherries, pipes removed
½ apple skinned
½ tsp apple juice concentrate
½ cup plain yogurt

1 tsp caramel syrup
dash of nutmeg
dash of cinnamon
2 drops of vanilla essence
2 tsp cinnamon sugar
3 ice cubes

Place all ingredients except cinnamon in blender; blend until smooth. Pour into chilled glasses and serve topped with cinnamon sugar. Serves 2.

Apple Crumble Smoothie

½ cup milk
½ custard apple, pipes removed
½ banana
½ cup plain yogurt
1 tsp caramel syrup

¼ cup toasted granola
sprinkle of cinnamon and nutmeg
2 drops vanilla extract
1 tbsp coconut
3 ice cubes

Place all ingredients except coconut in blender; blend until smooth. Pour into chilled glasses and serve topped with toasted coconut. Serves 2.

Anzac Cookie Smoothie

Apple Cherry Pie Smoothie

Apple Crumble Smoothie

Apricot Danish Smoothie

Apricot Danish Smoothie

¼ cup milk
½ cup stewed or roasted apricots,
  chilled
¼ cup plain yogurt
¼ cup Philadelphia cream cheese
¼ cup apricot nectar

½ tsp honey
2–3 drops vanilla extract
dash of nutmeg
dash of cinnamon
4 ice cubes

Place all ingredients except spices in blender; blend until smooth.
Pour into chilled glasses and serve topped with cinnamon and nutmeg.
Serves 2.

Banana Berry Muffin Smoothie

½ cup milk
½ banana
12 blueberries
½ cup plain yogurt
2 tsps toffee syrup

2 tsps ground almond spread
2–3 drops vanilla extract
pinch of cinnamon and nutmeg
extra blueberries to garnish
4 ice cubes

Place all ingredients in blender; blend until smooth. Pour into chilled
glasses and serve topped with a scatter of blueberries. Serves 2.

Banana Cherry Split Smoothie

½ cup milk
1 banana
6 cherries, pips removed
1 tbsp strawberry jelly
1 tbsp chocolate syrup

½ cup plain yogurt
2–3 drops vanilla extract
small chocolate buttons to garnish
4 ice cubes

Place all ingredients except garnish in blender; blend until smooth. Pour
into chilled glasses and serve topped with chocolate buttons. Serves 2.

Banana Berry Muffin Smoothie

Banana Cherry Split Smoothie

Banana Choc Nut Smoothie

½ cup milk

1 banana

2 tbsp chocolate syrup

2 tbsp hazelnut paste

½ cup plain yogurt

1 tsp honey

2–3 drops vanilla extract

pinch of nutmeg

4 ice cubes

Place all ingredients except nutmeg in blender; blend until smooth. Pour into chilled glasses and serve topped with nutmeg. Serves 2.

Banana Pudding Smoothie

½ cup milk

1 banana

½ cup plain yogurt

½ tsp caramel syrup

½ tsp toffee syrup

2–3 drops vanilla extract

4 ice cubes

1 tbsp toasted coconut

pinch of nutmeg

Place all ingredients in blender; blend until smooth. Pour into chilled glasses and serve topped with toasted coconut. Serves 2.

Banario Smoothie

½ cup milk

1 banana

2 chocolate biscuits, crushed

⅓ cup plain yogurt

4 ice cubes

extra biscuit, crushed to garnish

Place all ingredients except garnish in blender; blend until smooth. Pour into chilled glasses and serve topped with half a chocolate biscuit. Serves 2.

Banana Choc Nut Smoothie

Banana Pudding Smoothie

Banario Smoothie

Cheesecake Smoothie

Cheesecake Smoothie

½ cup milk
½ cup custard apple, seeds removed
¼ cup Philadelphia cream
  cheese
¼ cup plain yogurt
1 tsp caramel syrup

2 tsps hazelnut spread
2 drops vanilla extract
sprinkle of nutmeg
extra caramel syrup to garnish
4 ice cubes

Place all ingredients except topping in blender; blend until smooth.
Pour into chilled glasses and serve topped with a swirl of caramel
syrup. Serves 2.

Cherry Ripe Smoothie

10 frozen cherries, depipped
½ cup plain yogurt
½ cup coconut milk

2 tsps dark chocolate syrup
2 ice cubes

Place all ingredients except toppings in blender; blend until smooth.
Pour in ½ cup of coconut milk and stir. Pour into chilled glasses and
serve topped with a cherry and a swirl of chocolate syrup. Serves 2.

Choc Berry Smoothie

½ cup milk
4 strawberries, frozen
8–10 blueberries
½ cup plain yogurt
1 tbsp chocolate syrup

2–3 drops vanilla extract
extra chocolate syrup to garnish
1 extra strawberry to garnish
3 ice cubes

Place all ingredients in blender; blend until smooth. Pour into chilled
glasses and serve topped with half a strawberry and a swirl of syrup.
Serves 2.

Cherry Ripe Smoothie

Choc Berry Smoothie

Choc Mint Berry Smoothie

½ cup milk
½ banana
3 strawberries
2 tsps choc mint syrup

½ cup plain yogurt
extra yogurt to garnish
1 tsp strawberry jelly
4 ice cubes

Place all ingredients except toppings in blender; blend until smooth.
Pour into chilled glasses and serve topped with an extra yogurt and
coloured sprinkles. Serves 2.

Honey Smack Smoothie

½ cup milk
½ cup custard apple, deseeded
1 weetbix or ¾ cup
  frosted mini wheats
¼ cup plain yogurt

2 tbsp honey
2–3 drops vanilla extract
extra cereal and honey
2 ice cubes

Place all ingredients except toppings in blender; blend until smooth.
Pour into chilled glasses and serve topped with lots of crushed cereal
and a dollop of honey. Serves 2.

Honeydew Heaven

½ cup diced cantaloupe
½ cup lime-flavoured drink
1 tsp lime juice

1 tbsp white sugar
1 large slice of cantaloupe, to garnish
6 ice cubes

Place all ingredients except lime soft drink and slice of cantaloupe in
blender; blend until smooth. Divide mixture between 2 glasses. Scoop
out 3 to 4 balls of cantaloupe flesh, place in each glasses top up with
lime-flavoured drink and give a gentle stir. Serves 2.

Choc Mint Berry Smoothie

Honey Smack Smoothie

Honeydew Heaven

Iced Vovo Smoothie

Iced Vovo Smoothie

½ cup milk
¼ cup coconut milk
½ custard apple, deseeded
2 strawberries
½ cup plain yogurt

1 tsp raspberry jelly
2 tsps macadamia paste
2 drops vanilla extract
toasted coconut to garnish
2 ice cubes

Place all ingredients except coconut in blender; blend until smooth.
Pour into chilled glasses and serve topped with toasted coconut.
Serves 2.

Jaffa Smoothie

¼ cup milk
½ banana
juice of 1 orange
½ cup plain yogurt

2 tsps chocolate syrup
2–3 drops vanilla extract
chocolate curls for topping
2 ice cubes

Place all ingredients except topping in blender; blend until smooth. Pour
into chilled glasses and serve topped with chocolate curls. Serves 2.

Lemon Meringue Smoothie

¼ cup milk
½ banana
2 tbsps lemon butter
2 tsps caramel syrup

½ cup plain yogurt
2–3 drops vanilla extract
toasted coconut for topping
4 ice cubes

Place all ingredients except topping in blender; blend until smooth. Pour
in ¼ cup of coconut milk and stir. Pour into chilled glasses and serve
topped with toasted coconut. Serves 2.

Jaffa Smoothie

Lemon Meringue Smoothie

Luscious Lime Pie Smoothie

½ cup milk
1 kiwifruit, peeled
2 tbsps lemon butter
½ cup plain yogurt
1 squeeze lime juice

1 tsp caramel syrup
2–3 drops vanilla extract
pinch of nutmeg
pinch of cinnamon
3 ice cubes

Place all ingredients except spices in blender; blend until smooth. Pour into chilled glasses and serve topped with a sprinkle of cinnamon and nutmeg. Serves 2.

Monte Carlo Smoothie

½ cup milk
½ custard apple, deseeded
½ banana
2 tsps macadamia paste
½ cup plain yogurt

1 tsp raspberry jelly
2–3 drops vanilla extract
sprinkle of nutmeg
1 crushed malt biscuit for topping
2 ice cubes

Place all ingredients except biscuit in blender; blend until smooth. Pour into chilled glasses and serve sprinkled with a crushed malt biscuit. Serves 2.

Muesli (Granola) Bar Smoothie

½ cup milk
½ banana
2 tbsps muesli (granola)
2 tsps date pulp
½ cup plain yogurt

½ tsp molasses
2–3 drops vanilla extract
extra muesli (granola) for topping
3 ice cubes

Place all ingredients except topping in blender; blend until smooth. Pour into chilled glasses and serve topped with a sprinkle of granola. Serves 2.

Lucious Lime Pie Smoothie

Monte Carlo Smoothie

Muesli (Granola) Bar Smoothie

Peanut Butter and Jelly Smoothie

Peanut Butter and Jelly Smoothie

½ cup milk
½ banana
4 strawberries
4 tbsps peanut butter

½ cup plain yogurt
1 tsp strawberry jelly
extra peanut butter for topping
4 ice cubes

Place all ingredients except topping in blender; blend until smooth. Pour into chilled glasses and serve topped with a dollop of peanut butter. Serves 2.

Pear and Coconut Delight Smoothie

½ cup milk
½ cup stewed or roasted pear, chilled
½ cup plain yogurt
1 tsp honey
2 tbsps of toasted coconut

1 tsp pear concentrate
2 drops vanilla extract
extra yogurt for topping
4 ice cubes

Place all ingredients except topping in blender; blend until smooth. Pour into chilled glasses and serve topped with an extra dollop of yogurt and a sprinkle of toasted coconut. Serves 2.

Pear Danish Smoothie

½ cup milk
½ cup stewed or roasted pear, chilled
½ cup plain yogurt
¼ cup Philadelphia cream cheese
½ tsp pear juice concentrate
½ tsp toffee-flavoured syrup

2–3 drops vanilla extract
1 Italian finger biscuit for topping
2 tsp honey
dash of nutmeg
4 ice cubes

Place all ingredients except biscuit, honey and nutmeg in blender; blend until smooth. Serve in chilled glasses, topped with crushed biscuit, an extra dollop of yogurt and a drizzle of honey. Serves 2.

Pear and Coconut Delight Smoothie

Pear Danish Smoothie

Raspberry ✪ Orange Delight (image page 12)

½ cup fresh or unsweetened frozen raspberries
½ cups orange juice
1 tbsp honey
½ cups lemon-lime soda
10 ice blocks

Blend raspberries, orange juice, honey. Put 5 ice blocks in each glass, add about half a cup of the raspberry mixture, then add a dash of the soda to each glasses.

Strawberry Shortcake Smoothie

½ cup milk
6–8 strawberries
½ cup plain yogurt
1 tsp toffee-flavoured syrup
1 tsp caramel-flavoured syrup
2 drops vanilla extract
toasted coconut to garnish
dash of nutmeg
dash of cinnamon
4 ice cubes

Place all ingredients except spices and coconut in blender; blend until smooth. Pour into chilled glasses and serve topped with toasted coconut. Serves 2.

Strawberry Shortcake Smoothie

Strawberry Swirl

Strawberry Swirl

1 cup milk
4 tbsps strawberry syrup
4 frozen strawberries
dash of cinnamon
1 ice cube

Put all ingredients except the milk and 2 tablespoons of strawberry topping into a blender and blend until an icy puree is formed. Place in a small bowl and put into the freezer while you make the rest of the drink. Do not bother rinsing the blender. Add 1 cup of milk and 2 tablespoons of strawberry topping to blender and blend until frothy. Spoon half the frozen pulp into the bottom of each glass and drizzle a dash of syrup around the sides. Top up with strawberry milkshake and serve. Serves 2.

Toffee Apple Smoothie

½ cup milk
½ apple, skinned, cored and sliced into small pieces
1 tsp apple juice concentrate
4 cherries, de-pipped
½ cup plain yogurt
1 tsp toffee-flavoured syrup
1 tsp caramel-flavoured syrup
2–3 drops vanilla extract
coloured sprinkles to garnish
4 ice cubes

Place all ingredients except sprinkles in blender; blend until smooth. Pour into chilled glasses and serve topped with coloured sprinkles. Serves 2.

Toffee Apple Smoothie

For The Curious

Black Forest Gateau Smoothie **84**
Cantaloupe Cooler **84**
Cherry Fruit Cake Smoothie **84**
Cranberry Zinger **89**
Lime Egg Cream **89**
Liquado Mexicano **89**
Spicy Banana Flip **92**
Tiramisu Smoothie **92**

Black Forest Gateau Smoothie

1/4 cup milk
1/4 cup cream
1/2 cup plain yogurt
3 tsps black cherry jelly
1 tbsp chocolate syrup

3 cherries, pips removed
1/2 banana or 1/2 custard apple, deseeded
2–3 drops vanilla extract
chocolate curls
4 ice cubes

Place all ingredients except chocolate curls in blender; blend until smooth. Pour into chilled glasses and serve topped with a chocolate curls. Serves 2.

Cantaloupe Cooler

1 cup cantaloupe pieces
1 tbsp orange juice
1 tsp lemon juice

2 tsps white sugar
1 cup 7-up
2 ice blocks

Blend cantaloupe until liquefied. Pour half into tall glasses filled with ice and top up with 7-up. Serves 6.

Cherry Fruit Cake Smoothie

1/2 cup milk
1/4 apple
4 blueberries
2 cherries
1/2 banana
1/2 cup plain yogurt
1/2 tsp caramel syrup

1/2 tsp toffee-flavoured syrup
1 tbsp date spread
2 drops vanilla extract
extra berries for topping
dash of nutmeg
3 ice cubes

Place all ingredients except berries and nutmeg in blender; blend until smooth. Pour into chilled glasses and serve topped with berries. Serves 2.

Black Forest Gateau Smoothie

Cantaloupe Cooler

Cherry Fruit Cake Smoothie

Cranberry Zinger

Cranberry Zinger

½ cup cranberry juice
2 tsps brown sugar
1 tsp lemon extract
1 cup pineapple pieces (approximately 5oz/150g)
1 cup ginger ale

Combine all ingredients except ginger ale. Just add ginger ale and ice before serving. Serves 2.

Lime Egg Cream

1½ cups milk
½ lime soft drink
4 tbsps chocolate syrup

Pour half the milk into each cup. Top with the lime soda so that the foam reaches the top of the glass. Place a spoon in the glass. Add 2 tablespoons of the chocolate syrup per glass hitting the bottom of the spoon if possible. Beat quickly a few times to blend the syrup into the milk without deflating the foam Serves 2.

Liquado Mexicano

½ cup uncooked white rice
1 sticks cinnamon
¼ cup slivered almonds
2 cups water
2 tbsps honey
2–3 drops vanilla extract
½ cup plain yogurt

Grind rice to a coarse meal in a blender. Mix together rice, cinnamon, almonds and water. Cover loosely and let stand overnight. Purée the rice mixture, then strain. Return to blender, Mix in honey, vanilla extract and yogurt. Blend until smooth and serve. Serves 2.

Lime Egg Cream

Liquado Mexicano

Spicy Banana Flip

1½ cups milk
1 banana
3 pinches cinnamon
pinch of nutmeg
pinch of ground cloves

extra pinch of nutmeg to garnish
pinch of powdered cardamom
1 raw egg yolk
2 tsps honey
4 ice cubes

Place all ingredients in blender; blend until smooth. Pour into chilled glass and serve topped with a sprinkle of nutmeg. Serves 2.

Tiramisu Smoothie

½ cup milk
½ tsp decaffeinated instant
 coffee granules
1 banana
2 Italian finger biscuits, crushed

½ cup plain yogurt
½ tsp chocolate syrup
2–3 drops vanilla extract
4 ice cubes

Place all ingredients except 1 biscuit in blender; blend until smooth. Pour into chilled glass and serve topped with more crushed biscuit. Serves 2.

Spicy Banana Flip

Tiramisu Smoothie

Party Snacks

Cheese Triangles **96**
Cheesy Swirls **99**
Chicken Dipped in Sesame Seeds **100**
Chicken Nuggets **103**
Corn Plants **104**
Crunchy Cutlets **107**
Honey-glazed Spareribs **108**
Sausage Puffs **111**
Speedy Lasagne **112**
Apple Crumble **115**
Apple Roll-ups **116**
Fruit and Jelly Wedges **119**
Lamingtons **120**
Syrup Bananas **123**

Cheese Triangles

10 oz/300g ricotta cheese
10 oz/300g feta cheese
4 eggs
white pepper
1 packet filo pastry
4 oz/125g melted butter

Pre-heat oven to 400°F/200°C. Combine the ricotta, feta and eggs in a bowl and mix well. Season with pepper. Brush one layer of filo pastry with melted butter, and place another layer on top. Cut the pastry, lengthwise, into 4 strips. To shape the triangles, place a heaped teaspoon of cheese mixture close to the bottom of the right hand corner of the strip. Fold this corner, diagonally across to the left-hand edge over the mixture to form a triangle. Continue folding from right to left in a triangular shape to the end of strip. Brush top of triangle with the melted butter and place on a baking tray. Repeat until all mixture has been used. Bake triangles in the oven for about 20 minutes or until they are golden. Makes 4.

Cheese Triangles

Cheesy Swirls

Cheesy Swirls

14 oz/400g shortcrust pastry
3$\frac{1}{2}$ oz/100g mature cheddar, grated
2 tbsps freshly grated Parmesan cheese
2 tbsps tomato purée
$\frac{1}{2}$ tsp sugar
all-purpose flour for dusting
1 medium egg, beaten, for glazing
vegetable oil for greasing

Preheat the oven to 375°F/190°C. Roll out the pastry on a floured surface and cut to make 2 rectangles measuring 8 x 10 in/20 x 25cm. Mix together the cheddar and Parmesan, then set aside. Spread 1 sheet of pastry with the tomato purée mixed with the half teaspoon of sugar. Place the second sheet of pastry on top, then sprinkle with the cheese. Roll up the pastry from the shorter side with the filling inside. Brush the roll with the egg and refrigerate for 20 minutes. Cut the roll into 1cm slices and place on greased baking sheets. Bake for 20 minutes or until golden. Leave on wire racks to cool slightly. Makes 10.

Chicken Dipped in Sesame Seeds

1 lb/500g chicken tenderloins
$\frac{1}{4}$ tsp sesame oil
$\frac{1}{4}$ tsp five spice powder
2 tbsp cornstarch, for dusting
peanut oil
3 tbsps honey
1 tbsp lemon juice
2 tbsps sesame seeds

Batter
1 oz/30g cornstarch
3 oz/85g all-purpose flour
1 tsp baking soda
$10\frac{1}{2}$ oz/300mL water
1 egg white

Cut tenderloins in half. Mix with sesame oil and five spice powder and stand 15 minutes. To make the batter, sift the cornstarch and baking soda into a bowl. Add water and mix until free of lumps. Beat egg white until stiff, and fold into the batter. Place oil in wok to heat. Dip a piece of chicken into the cornstarch shake off excess, dip into the batter and place immediately into the hot oil. Repeat with 5 or 6 more pieces. Cook until golden brown, then place on a tray lined with absorbent paper. Repeat with remainder. Drain all the oil from the wok. Add honey and lemon juice to the wok and heat through on medium heat. Add chicken a few pieces at a time, coat with honey mixture, remove to a serving platter and sprinkle with sesame seeds. Serve hot. Serves 4.

Chicken Dipped in Sesame

Chicken Nuggets

Chicken Nuggets

1lb/500g ground chicken
1 egg, lightly beaten
1$\frac{1}{2}$ oz/45g breadcrumbs, made from
stale bread
2 oz/60g cottage cheese, mashed
4 oz/125g dried breadcrumbs
vegetable oil for shallow frying

Place ground chicken, egg, soft breadcrumbs and cottage cheese in a
bowl and mix well to combine. Take 2 tablespoons of mixture, shape
into a ball, then flatten slightly and gently press into dried breadcrumbs
to coat. Repeat until all remaining mixture is used. Heat $\frac{1}{2}$ in/1cm oil
in a frying pan over a medium heat until hot, add nuggets and cook
for 2 minutes each side or until cooked through and golden. Drain on
absorbent paper, cool slightly and serve. Makes 24.

Corn Plants

3 red bell peppers
3 yellow bell peppers
3 tbsps balsamic vinegar
½ cup olive oil
6 baby corn cobs
1 large onion, chopped
2 cloves garlic, chopped
7 oz/200g ground lamb
3 tsps tomato paste
3 oz/90g bulgur (cracked wheat)
2 cups lamb stock
3 oz/90g frozen peas
3 oz/90g dried apricots, chopped
3 tsps ground coriander
black pepper
watercress sprigs to garnish

Preheat oven to 400°F/200°C. Slice off and discard the tops of the peppers and deseed. Square off the bottoms and stand on a baking tray lined with a sheet of baking paper. Sprinkle with the balsamic vinegar and 1 tablespoon of the oil. Cook for 15 minutes then add the baby corn to the sheet. Cook for 5–10 minutes, until everything is tender. Meanwhile, heat the remaining oil in a large saucepan, add the onion and garlic and fry for 5 minutes or until softened. Add the ground lamb and cook for 5 minutes on a low heat or until browned. Stir in the tomato paste, bulgur, stock, peas, apricots and coriander, then season. Bring to the boil, then simmer for 15 minutes or until the stock has been absorbed. Stir occasionally. Place the peppers on plates and fill with the lamb mixture. Insert a baby corn cob and decorate a few watercress sprigs on the top of each one. Serves 6.

Corn Plants

Crunchy Cutlets

Crunchy Cutlets

6 lamb cutlets, trimmed and slightly flattened
1 tbsp vegetable oil

Crunchy coating
1 egg, lightly beaten
¾ cup breadcrumbs, made from stale bread
1 oz/30g cornflakes, crushed

Place egg in a shallow dish. Place breadcrumbs and crushed cornflakes in a separate dish and mix to combine. Dip cutlets in egg, then in breadcrumb mixture to coat. Heat oil in a frying pan over a medium heat until hot, add cutlets and cook for 2 minutes on each side or until cooked through and golden. Serves 6.

Honey-glazed Spareribs

4 lb/2 kg pork spareribs, trimmed of excess fat
2 tbsps orange juice
4 oz/125g butter, melted

Honey soy marinade
1 cups rice
Chinese white vinegar
½ cup reduced-salt
soy sauce
½ cup honey

To make marinade, combine vinegar, soy sauce and honey in a non-reactive dish. Add ribs, toss to coat, cover and marinate in the refrigerator for at least 4 hours. Drain ribs and reserve marinade. Cook ribs, on a preheated hot barbecue grill for 8–10 minutes or until ribs are tender and golden basting occasionally with reserved marinade. Place on a serving platter, cover and keep warm. Place remaining marinade in a saucepan, add orange juice and bring to the boil. Reduce heat and simmer for 15 minutes or until sauce reduces by half. Pour sauce over spareribs. Serves 8.

Honey Glazed Spareribs

Sausage Puffs

Sausage Puffs

12 oz/340g prepared puff pastry
curried sausage filling
12 oz/340g sausage meat
1 small carrot, finely grated
1 tbsp fruit chutney
1 tsp curry powder
freshly ground black pepper
salt

To make filling, place meat, carrot, chutney, salt and black pepper to taste in a bowl and mix to combine. Cover and refrigerate until required. Roll out pastry to $1/8$ in/3 mm thick and cut out a 12 in/30 cm square. Cut pastry square in half. Divide filling into two equal portions then shape each into a thin sausage about 12 in/30cm long. Place a sausage on the long edge of each pastry rectangle and roll up. Brush edges with water to seal. Cut each roll into $1/2$ in/1 cm thick slices, place on greased baking trays and bake for 12–15 minutes or until filling is cooked and pastry is golden and puffed. Makes 48.

Note: These savoury puffs can be prepared to the baking stage earlier in the day. Cover with plastic food wrap and store in the refrigerator until required, then bake as directed in the recipe.

Speedy Lasagne

3 oz/90g packet white sauce mix
12 instant lasagne sheets (no precooking required)
3 oz/90g mature cheddar cheese, grated

Spicy meat sauce
2 tsps vegetable oil
1 onion, finely chopped
1 clove garlic, crushed
1 lb/500g lean ground beef
16 fl oz/500mL jar pasta sauce

To make meat sauce, heat oil in a frying pan over a medium heat, add onion and garlic and cook for 2 minutes or until onion is soft. Add ground beef and cook, stirring, for 5 minutes longer or until meat is brown. Add pasta sauce, bring to simmering and simmer for 2 minutes. Set aside. Make white sauce according to packet directions. Place 4 lasagne sheets in the base of a lightly greased ovenproof dish. Top with one-third of the meat sauce, then one-third of the white sauce and 4 lasagne sheets. Repeat layers, finishing with a layer of white sauce. Sprinkle with cheese and bake for 20–25 minutes or until hot and bubbling and top is golden. Serves 4.

Speedy Lasagne

Apple Crumble

Apple Crumble

3 apples

Crumble topping
¾ cup brown sugar
½ cup plain flour
¾ cup rolled oats
2 oz/60g butter

Preheat oven to 350°F/180°C. Cut apples into quarters. Peel and cut out cores. Slice thinly. Place apple slices in lightly buttered ovenproof dish. Make topping. Place sugar, flour and rolled oats in bowl. Chop butter into pieces. Add to bowl. Using your fingers, mix in butter until mixture is crumbly. Sprinkle topping over apples. Bake for 35 minutes. Serves 6.

Apple Roll-ups

2 oz/60g plain flour
5 fl oz/150mL full-fat milk
1 medium egg
rind of 1 orange, finely grated
1 oz/30g butter, melted, plus extra for frying
maple syrup to serve

For the filling

2 eating apples, peeled, cored and chopped
½ tsp ground cinnamon
1 tbsp water

To make the batter, blend the flour, milk, egg, orange rind and melted
butter until smooth in a food processor or by using a hand blender.
Leave the mixture to rest for 20 minutes. Meanwhile, make the filling.
Put the apples, cinnamon and 1 tablespoon of water into a small
saucepan, cover, and cook gently for 5–7 minutes, stirring occasionally,
until the apples have softened. Melt just enough butter to cover the
base of a 18cm non-stick frying pan. Pour in a quarter of the batter
and tilt the pan so that it covers the base. Cook for 1–2 minutes
on each side, until golden. Keep warm and repeat to make 3 more
pancakes, greasing the pan when necessary. Place 2 pancakes on each
plate. Fill with the apple mixture and carefully roll up. Serve with maple
syrup. Try them with a scoop of vanilla ice cream. Serves 2.

Apple Roll-ups

Fruit and Jelly Wedges

Fruit and Jelly Wedges

14 oz/440g canned fruit of your choice in unsweetened juice
2 tbsps gelatine dissolved in ½ cup hot water, cooled
food colouring of your choice (optional)
3–4 oranges

Drain canned fruit and reserve juice. Combine gelatine mixture and
reserved juice in a measuring jug and make up to 2 cups with water.
Add a few drops of food colouring, if desired. Stir well to combine,
then refrigerate until mixture just begins to thicken. Cut oranges in
half and scoop out pulp with a spoon, leaving orange shells intact.
Fold drained fruit into jelly and spoon mixture into orange shells. Place
shells on a tray and refrigerate for 2–3 hours or until jelly is set. To
serve, cut each jelly-filled orange shell into three wedges. Serves 6–8.

Lamingtons

1 butter or sponge cake, 7 x 11 in/18 x 28cm
1 lb/500g icing sugar
3 tbsps cocoa powder
6–8 tbsps warm water
1 lb/500g dried coconut

Cut sponge into twelve squares. Set aside. Place icing sugar and cocoa powder in sifter or sieve. Sift into large bowl. Stir in water until you have a runny icing. Pour icing into shallow cake tins. Place coconut in the another tin. Using tongs or two forks, dip cake squares in chocolate icing. Remove cake from icing. Allow excess icing to drain off. Roll in chocolate-coated coconut. Place lamingtons on wire rack to set.
Makes 12.

Lamingtons

Syrup Bananas

Syrup Bananas

2 oz/60g unsalted butter
⅓ cup brown sugar
½ tsp ground cinnamon
4 bananas, halved lengthwise
¼ cup banana-flavoured syrup
½ cup orange juice
4 scoops vanilla ice cream

Melt butter in a heavy-based saucepan over a medium heat, add sugar and cinnamon and cook, stirring, until sugar melts and mixture is combined. Stir in orange juice and banana-flavoured syrup. Cook for 5 minutes or until mixture is thick and syrupy. Add bananas and toss to coat with syrup. To serve, divide bananas and ice cream between serving plates and drizzle sauce from pan over ice cream. Serve immediately. Serves 4.

Notes

_____

_____

_____

_____

_____

_____

_____

_____

_____

_____

_____

_____

_____

Notes

Notes

_____

_____

_____

_____

_____

_____

_____

_____

_____

_____

_____

_____

Notes

_____

_____

_____

_____

_____

_____

_____

_____

_____

_____

_____

_____

_____

Index

Anzac Cookie Smoothie 46

Apple Cherry Pie Smoothie 46

Apple Crumble 115

Apple Crumble Smoothie 46

Apple Roll-ups 116

Apricot Danish Smoothie 51

Banana Berry Muffin Smoothie 51

Banana Cherry Split Smoothie 51

Banana Choc Nut Smoothie 54

Banana Pudding Smoothie 54

Banana Smoothie 14

Banana Zing Smoothie 19

Banapple Smoothie 14

Banario Smoothie 54

Banberry Smoothie 14

Berry Banana Smoothie 19

Black Forest Gateau Smoothie 84

Calypso Smoothie 19

Cantaloupe Cooler 84

Cheese Triangles 96

Cheesecake Smoothie 59

Cheesy Swirls 99

Cherry Fruit Cake Smoothie 84

Cherry Ripe Smoothie 59

Chicken Dipped in Sesame Seeds 100

Chicken Nuggets 103

Choc Berry Smoothie 59

Choc Mint Berry Smoothie 62

Corn Plants 104

Cranberry Zinger 89

Crunchy Cutlets 107

Custard Apple Smoothie 22

Fruit and Jelly Wedges 119

Fruit Salad Smoothie 22

Grape Slushie Swirl 22

Hawaiian Delight Smoothie 27

Honey-glazed Spareribs 108

Honey Smack Smoothie 62

Honeydew Heaven 62

Iced Vovo Smoothie 67

Jaffa Smoothie 67

Kiwi Frootz Smoothie 27

Lamingtons 120

Lemon Meringue Smoothie 67

Lime Egg Cream 89

Liquado Mexicano 89

Luscious Lime Pie Smoothie 70

Mango and Orange Smoothie 27

Mango Morning Smoothie 30

Melon Mix Smoothie 30

Monte Carlo Smoothie 70

Muesli Bar Smoothie 70

Passion Frootz 30

Peanut Butter and Jelly Smoothie 75

Pear and Coconut Delight Smoothie 75

Pear Danish Smoothie 75

Raspberry Orange Delight 78

Sausage Puffs 111

Speedy Lasagne 112

Spicy Banana Flip 92

Strawberry Orange Banana Smoothie 35

Strawberry Shortcake Smoothie 78

Strawberry Smoothie 35

Strawberry Swirl 81

Sunrise Surprise Smoothie 35

Syrup Bananas 123

Tiramisu Smoothie 92

Toffee Apple Smoothie 81

Tropical Burst Smoothie 38

Tropical Frootz Smoothie 38

Tropical Zing Smoothie 38

Tropicana Smoothie 43

Tropico Blitz 43